Billy Joel River of Dreams

Additional editing and transcription
by David Rosenthal

Cover Art: Christie Brinkley

ISBN 978-1-70513-601-0

Visit Hal Leonard Online at
www.halleonard.com

World headquarters, contact:
Hal Leonard
7777 West Bluemound Road
Milwaukee, WI 53213
Email: info@halleonard.com

In Europe, contact:
Hal Leonard Europe Limited
1 Red Place
London, W1K 6PL
Email: info@halleonardeurope.com

In Australia, contact:
Hal Leonard Australia Pty. Ltd.
4 Lentara Court
Cheltenham, Victoria, 3192 Australia
Email: info@halleonard.com.au

Released in 1993, *River of Dreams* was Billy Joel's 12th studio album. It entered the *Billboard* charts at #1, where it remained for three weeks, and has sold more than six million copies worldwide.

The album yielded four singles: "The River of Dreams," "All About Soul," "Lullabye," and "No Man's Land." The biggest hit was the title track, which peaked at #3 on the US charts and reached #1 in Australia and New Zealand. Its bouncy rhythm and singable gospel choir answers make the song a crowd favorite every time we play it live.

Having played keyboards in Billy Joel's band since 1993, I have an inside perspective into his music. Accordingly, Billy asked that I review every note of the sheet music in his entire catalog of songs. As a pianist myself, he entrusted me with the task of correcting and re-transcribing each piece to ensure that the printed music represents each song exactly as it was written and recorded. This is the latest edition in our series of revised songbooks in the Billy Joel catalog.

The challenge with each folio in Billy's catalog is to find musical ways to combine his piano parts and vocal melodies into playable piano arrangements. First, the signature piano parts are transcribed and notated exactly as Billy played them. The vocal melodies are then transcribed and incorporated into the piano part in a way that preserves the original character of each song. Billy's piano embellishments between his vocal phrases are also included wherever they are playable along with the vocal melodies.

All of the songs in this collection received the same astute attention to detail. The result is sheet music that is both accurate and enjoyable to play, and that remains true to the original performances.

Billy and I are pleased to present the revised and now accurate sheet music to the classic album *River of Dreams*.

Enjoy,

David Rosenthal
July 2022

BILLY JOEL
On the River of Dreams

Why the river? You know, what's this thing about rivers? There are spiritual and cultural meanings associated with rivers, and religions that worship rivers like the Ganges in India. Baptisms and Holy Water. Civilization began at the river delta of the Tigris and the Euphrates. Rivers beckoned the great explorers in days past. Can you imagine Henry Hudson sailing past the Palisades for the first time? Or Lewis and Clark seeing the Columbia River? The Mississippi inspired Mark Twain, one of our greatest American writers, so that Huck Finn and Tom Sawyer are as much a part of our heritage as the settlement at Jamestown (also on a river). So, there is this socio-historical thing. That's one side, but, as with all things, there's always another side.

And what is on the other side? This, I think, is the essence of the search in River of Dreams. In the dream I have, I go walking in my sleep, compelled because I've lost something intrinsic to my soul and I must find it. My quest takes me to many different places: the mountains of faith, which are the essence of belief and everything pure and good — the jungle of doubt, where nothing is clear and you've got to hack your way through it — the valley of fear, where you're surrounded by these towering outposts — the desert of truth, an arid, baked, caked place, where nothing lives. But each of these journeys ends at the river. And when I get there, I believe that what I am looking for is on the other side. I can't quite see it, it's not at all clear, but I know in my heart that it exists there. The river itself is wide and deep and daunting. And although I try to get across, ultimately I am carried along in it. The river becomes a metaphor for destiny. You can't possibly control it, but you can't stop yourself from trying to either. The best we can hope for is some kind of peace that comes with surrender, because the river was here before we were, and will be here long after we're gone. It's continuity: the cool, clear, cleansing, flowing, eternal river. The River of Dreams.

C O N T E N T S

NO MAN'S LAND

Words and Music by
BILLY JOEL

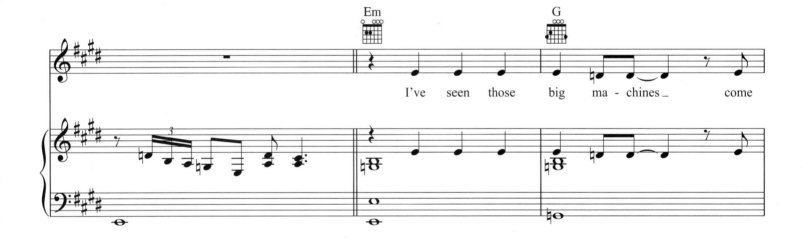

I've seen those big ma-chines _ come

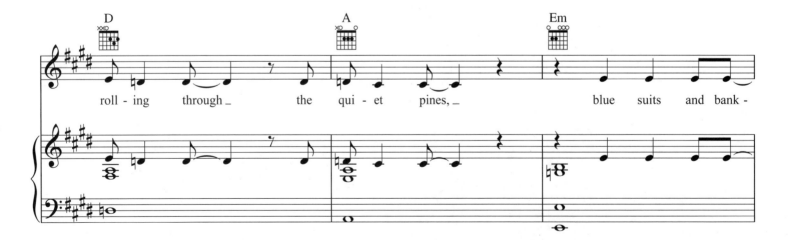

roll-ing through _ the qui-et pines, _ blue suits and bank-

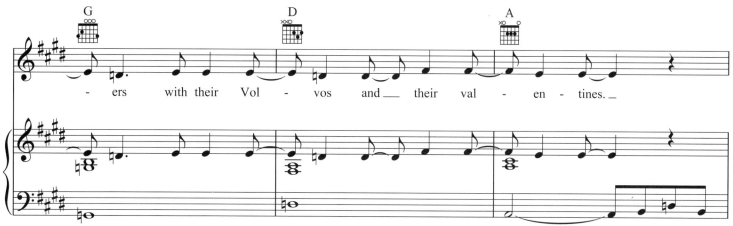

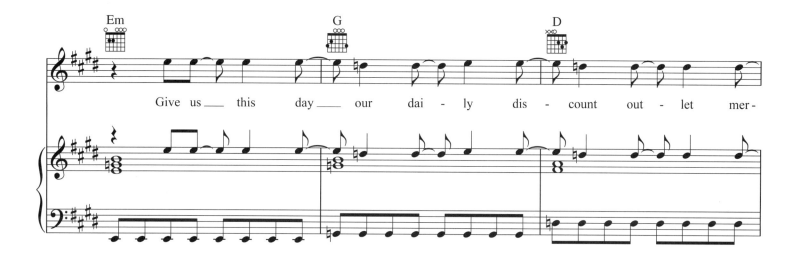

big bus - 'ness. Now we're gon - na get the real thing. _

Ev - 'ry - bod - y's all ex - cit - ed a - bout _ it. Who re - mem - bers when it

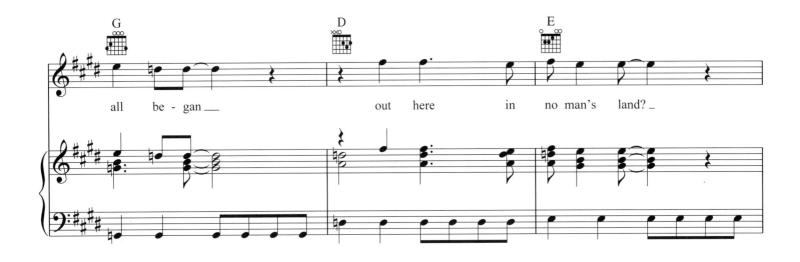

all be - gan _ out here in no man's land? _

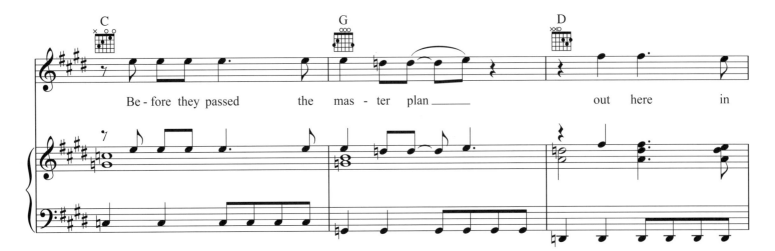

Be - fore they passed the mas - ter plan _ out here in

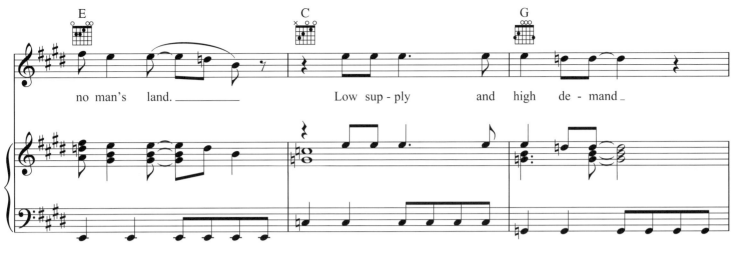

no man's land. _____ Low sup-ply and high de-mand _

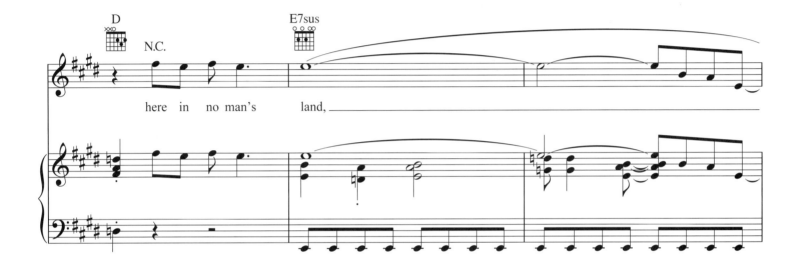

here in no man's land, _____

in no man's land.

There ain't __ much work __ out __ here __ in our con-sum - er pow-
I __ see these chil - dren with their bore - dom and their va -

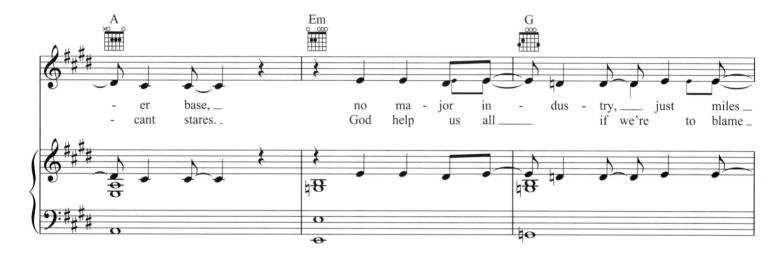

- er base, __ no ma - jor in - dus - try, __ just miles __
- cant stares. __ God help us all _____ if we're to blame __

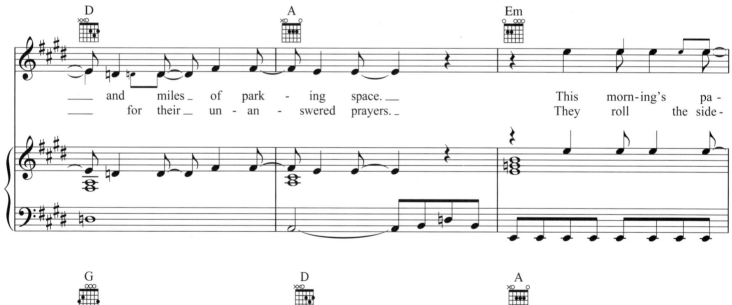

____ and miles __ of park - ing space. __ This morn-ing's pa -
____ for their __ un - an - swered prayers. __ They roll the side-

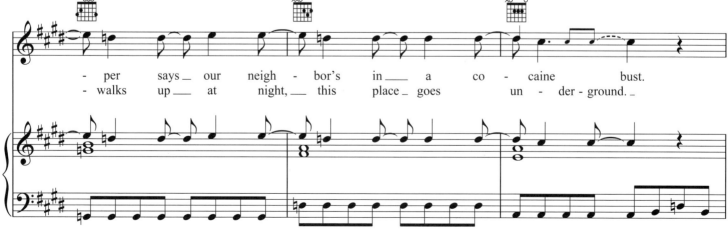

- per says __ our neigh - bor's in __ a co - caine bust.
- walks up __ at night, __ this place __ goes un - der - ground. __

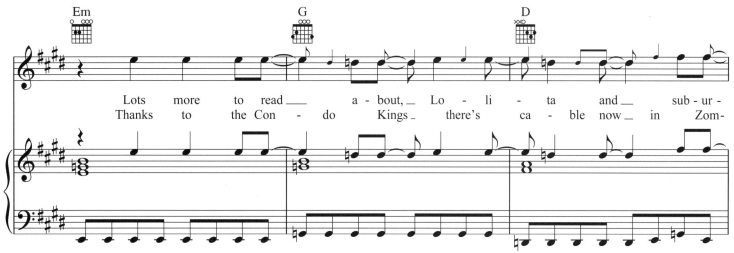

Lots more to read ___ a - bout, __ Lo - li - ta and __ sub - ur -
Thanks to the Con - do Kings __ there's ca - ble now __ in Zom -

- ban lust.
- bie - town. __

Now we're gon - na get the whole sto - ry.
Now we're gon - na get the closed cir - cuit.

To Coda ⊕

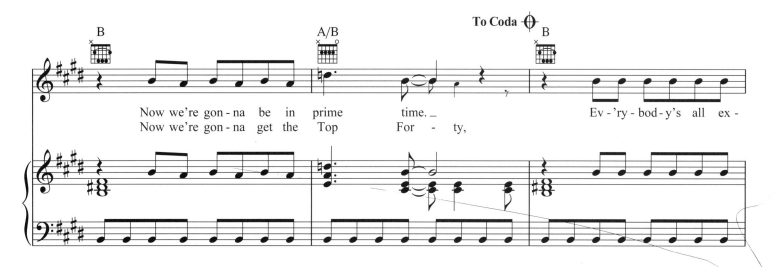

Now we're gon - na be in prime time. __
Now we're gon - na get the Top For - ty,

Ev - 'ry - bod - y's all ex -

- cit - ed a - bout __ it.
Who re - mem - bers when it all be - gan _____

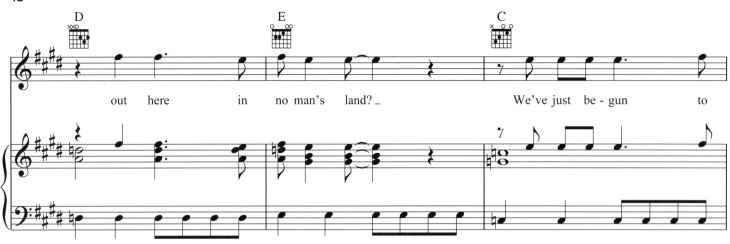

out here in no man's land? _ We've just be-gun to

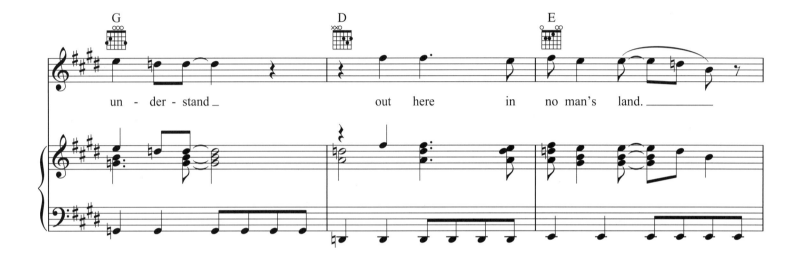

un-der-stand _ out here in no man's land. _____

Low sup-ply and high de-mand _ here in no man's

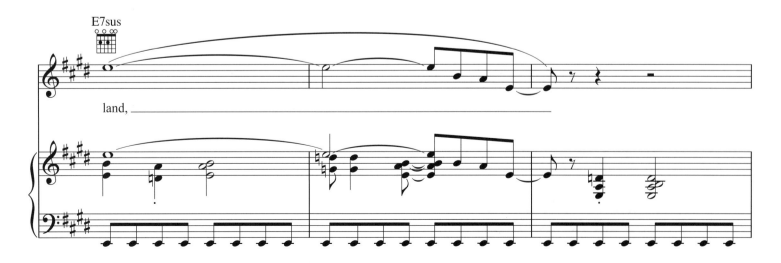

land, _____

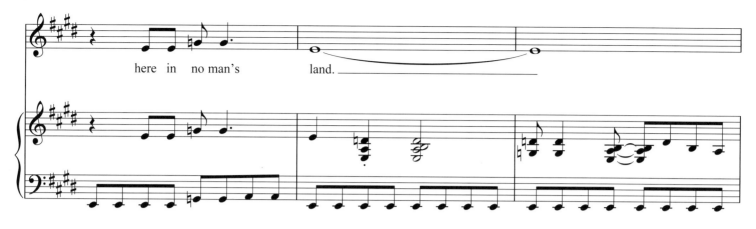

here in no man's land. _____

D.S. al Coda

CODA

B

Now we're gon-na get the

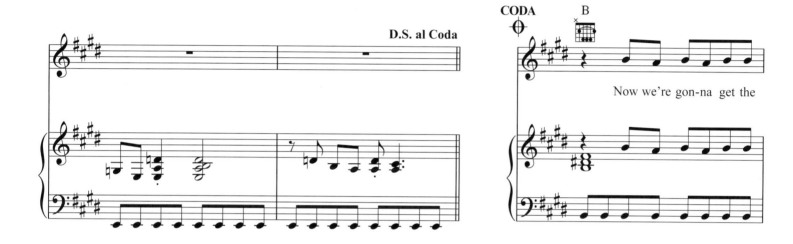

A/B

B

sports fran - chise. Now we're gon - na get the ma - jor at - trac - tions.

C

G

D

Who re - mem-bers when it all be - gan ___ out here in

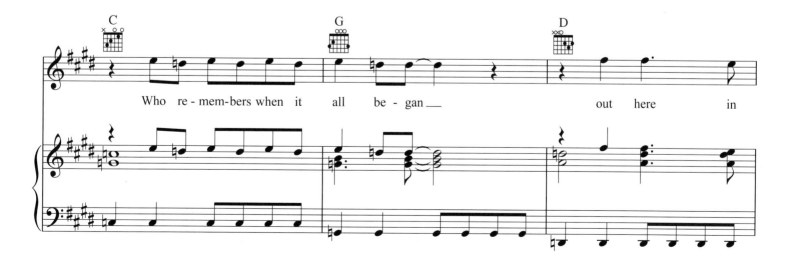

no man's land? _ Be - fore the whole world was in our hands _____

out here in no man's land; _____ be - fore the ban - ners and the

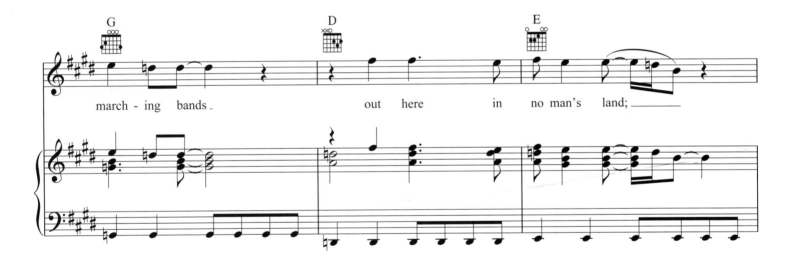

march - ing bands _ out here in no man's land; _____

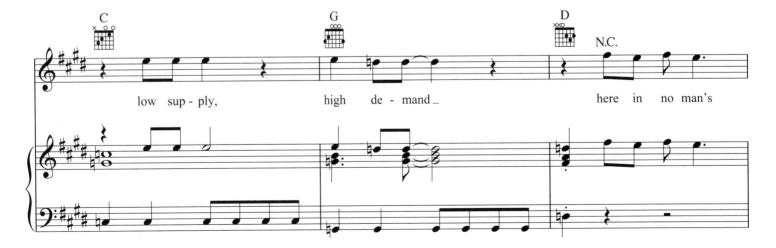

low sup - ply, high de - mand _ here in no man's

land;

here in no man's land;

here in no man's land;

Repeat and Fade

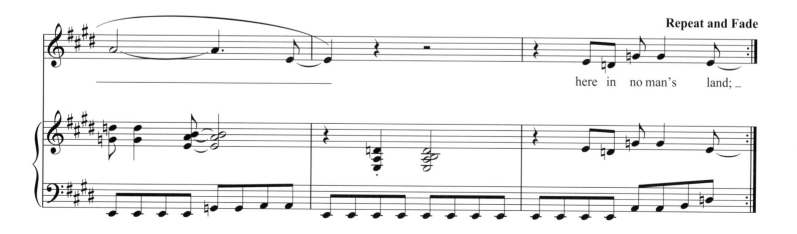

here in no man's land;

THE GREAT WALL OF CHINA

Words and Music by
BILLY JOEL

Moderate Rock

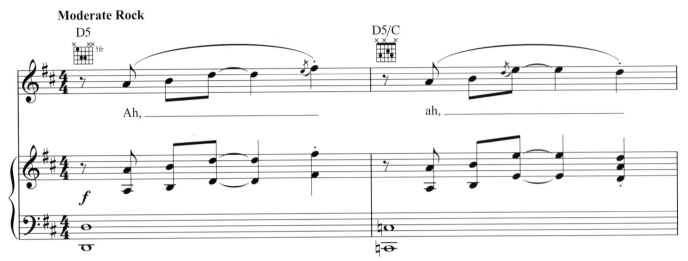

Ah,

ah,

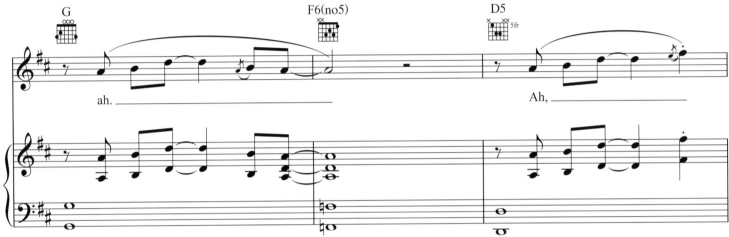

ah.

Ah,

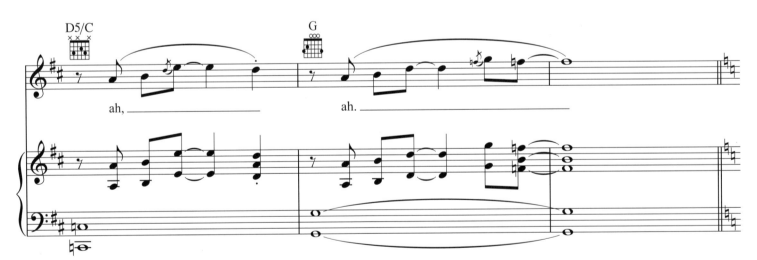

ah,

ah.

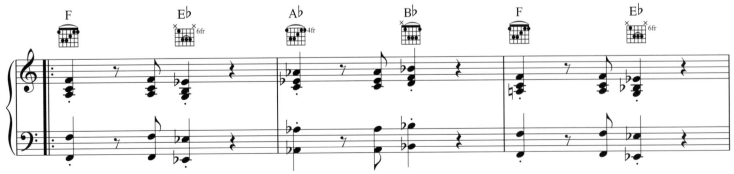

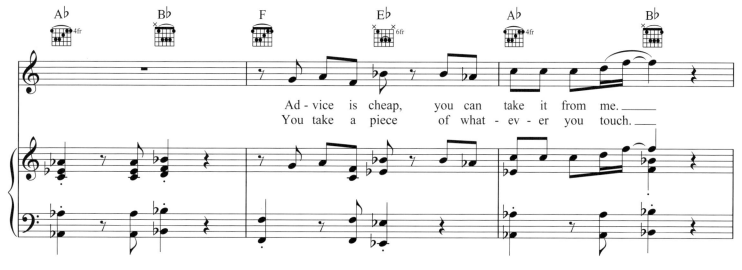

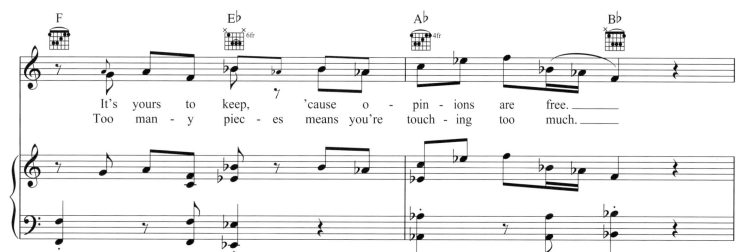

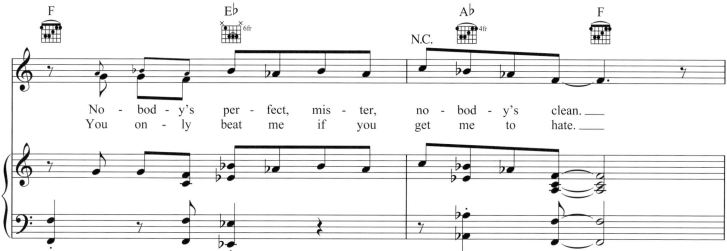

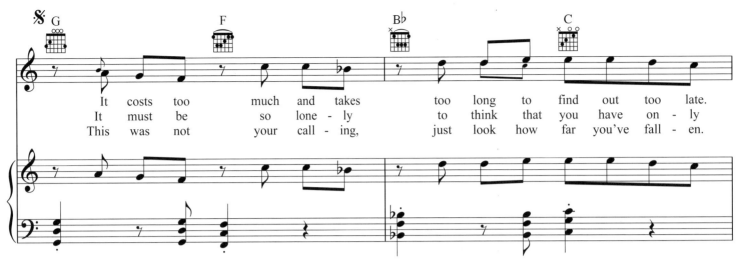

It costs too much and takes too long to find out too late.
It must be so lone - ly to think that you have on - ly
This was not your call - ing, just look how far you've fall - en.

Some words are not heard 'till af - ter they're spo - ken.
some - bod - y els - e's life to live if they let you.
I heard your sto - ry, man, you've got to be jok - ing.

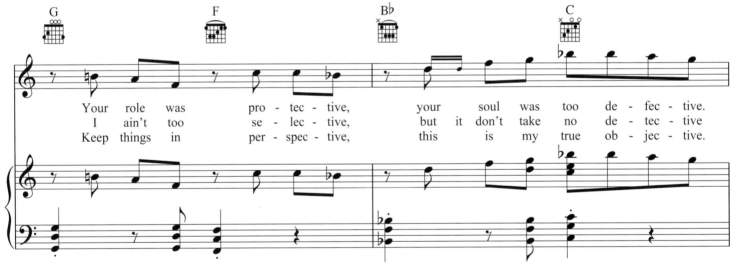

Your role was pro - tec - tive, your soul was too de - fec - tive.
I ain't too se - lec - tive, but it don't take no de - tec - tive
Keep things in per - spec - tive, this is my true ob - jec - tive.

Some peo - ple just don't have a heart to be bro - ken. __
to find out how fast your friends will for - get you. __
Why tear this heart out if it's on - ly been bro - ken? __

(1., 3.) We could have gone all the way __ to the Great Wall __ of Chi __ na __
(2.) We could have gone all the way __ to the Great Wall __ of Chi __ na. __

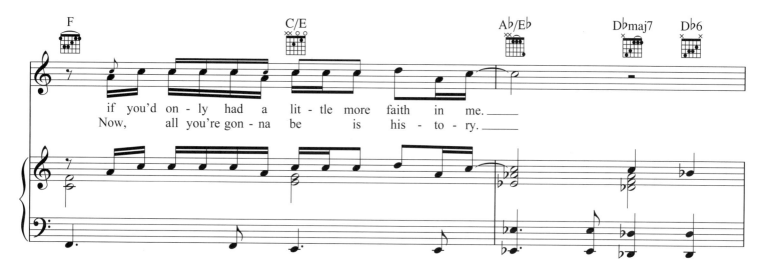

if you'd on - ly had a lit - tle more faith in me. _____
Now, all you're gon - na be is his - to - ry. _____

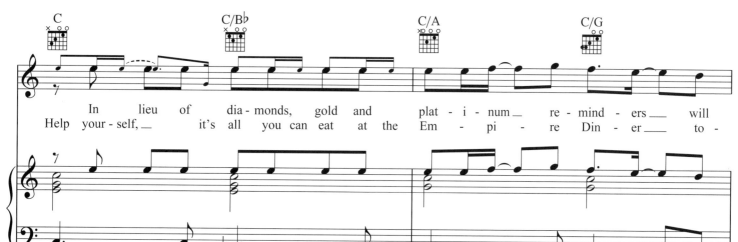

In lieu of dia - monds, gold and plat - i - num __ re - mind - ers __ will
Help your - self, __ it's all you can eat at the Em - pi - re Din - er __ to -

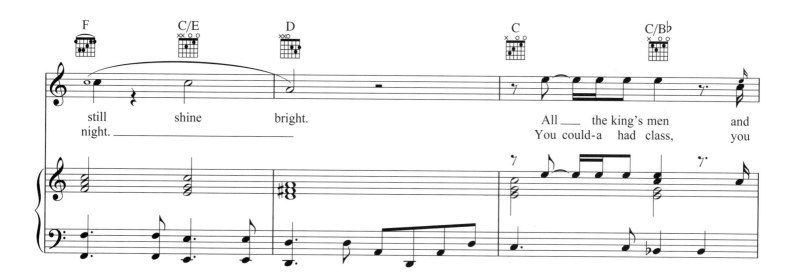

still shine bright.
night. _____ All __ the king's men and
You could-a had class, you

all the king's __ hors - es   can't   put you to - geth - er   the way   you   used   to   be. __
could - a   been ___ a con - tend - er.   Char - lie,   you   should-a looked   out   for   me. __

To Coda

__ We   could have been   stand - ing   on ___   the

Great   Wall __   of Chi - na. ___   You   could have been   stand - ing,

stand - ing   on __   the Great   Wall __   of Chi -   na.
Ah, _____

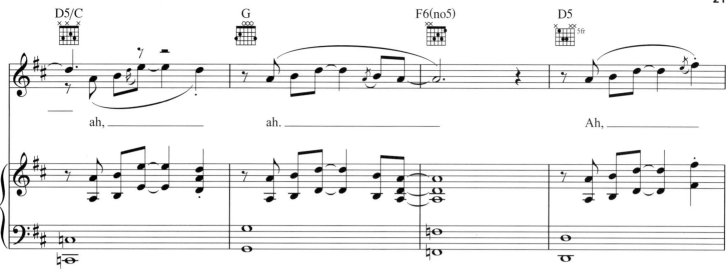

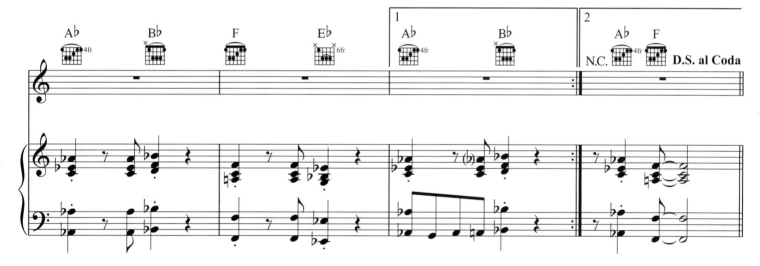

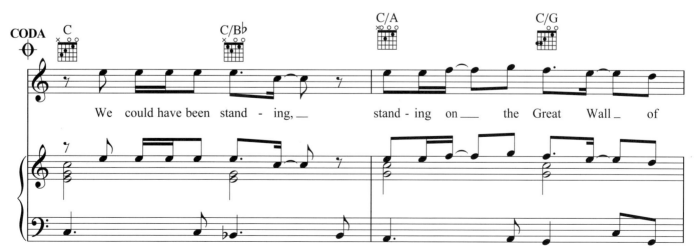

We could have been stand - ing, __ stand - ing on __ the Great Wall __ of

BLONDE OVER BLUE

Words and Music by
BILLY JOEL

Moderate Rock

Some days when I'm
These days there's a
These days not a

far a - way in a lone - ly room in a cold se - clu - sion;
mil - lion ways to be pulled and torn, to be mis - di - rect - ed.
damn soul prays and there is no faith, 'cause there's noth - ing to be - lieve in.

some nights when I'm wound so tight there is no re - lease, there is
These times there are sins and crimes on the morn - ing shows for the
These days on - ly good luck pays if we don't get paid then we

C5

no so - lu - tion. In hell there's a big ho - tel where the
dis - con - nect - ed. I look and I write my book and I
try to get e - ven. I look and I write my book and I

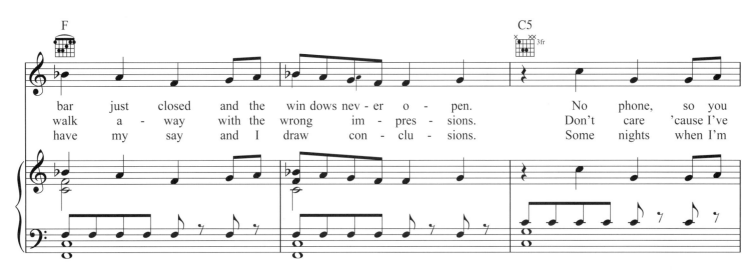

F   **C5**

bar just closed and the win dows nev - er o - pen. No phone, so you
walk a - way with the wrong im - pres - sions. Don't care 'cause I've
have my say and I draw con - clu - sions. Some nights when I'm

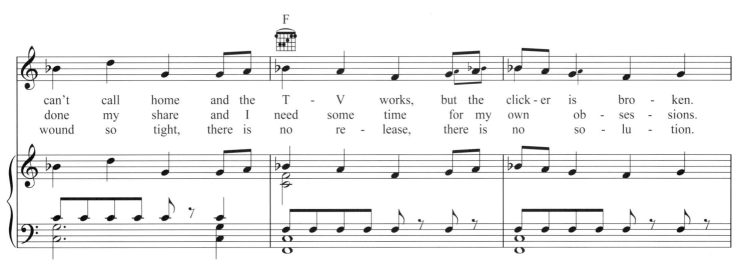

F

can't call home and the T - V works, but the click - er is bro - ken.
done my share and I need some time for my own ob - ses - sions.
wound so tight, there is no re - lease, there is no so - lu - tion.

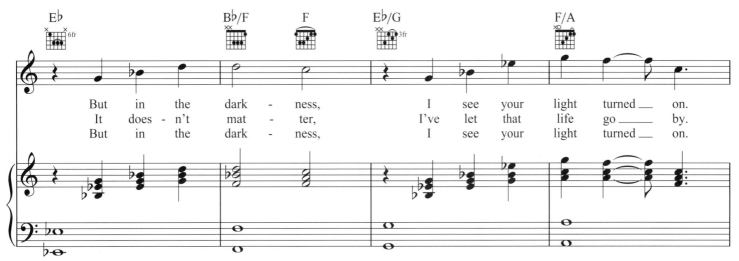

Eb   **Bb/F**   **F**   **Eb/G**   **F/A**

But in the dark - ness, I see your light turned __ on.
It does - n't mat - ter, I've let that life go _____ by.
But in the dark - ness, I see your life light turned __ on.

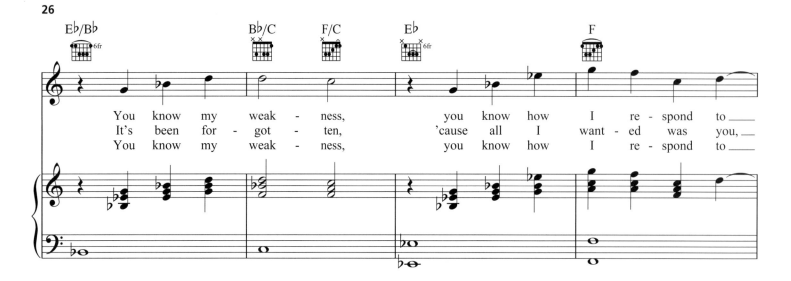

You know my weak - ness, you know how I re - spond to ____
It's been for - got - ten, 'cause all I want - ed was you, ____
You know my weak - ness, you know how I re - spond to ____

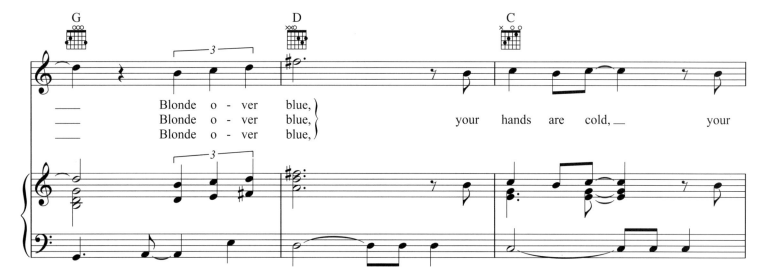

____ Blonde o - ver blue, your hands are cold, ____ your
____ Blonde o - ver blue,
____ Blonde o - ver blue,

eyes are fire. ____ Blonde o - ver blue, ____ they ____

____ shine as though you're burn - ing in - side. ____ One word from

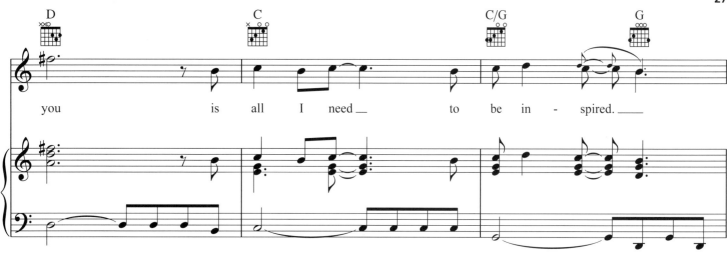

you is all I need ___ to be in - spired. ___

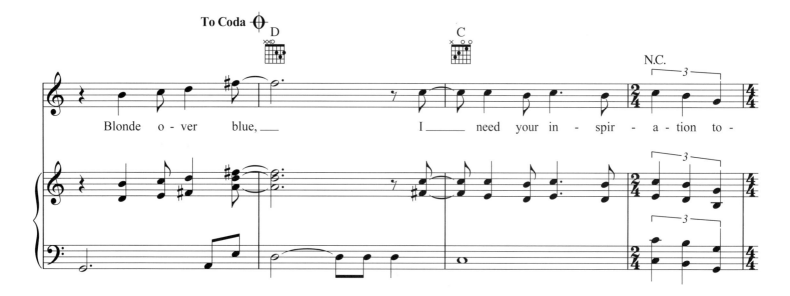

To Coda ⊕ D   C   N.C.

Blonde o - ver blue, ___ I ___ need your in - spir - a - tion to -

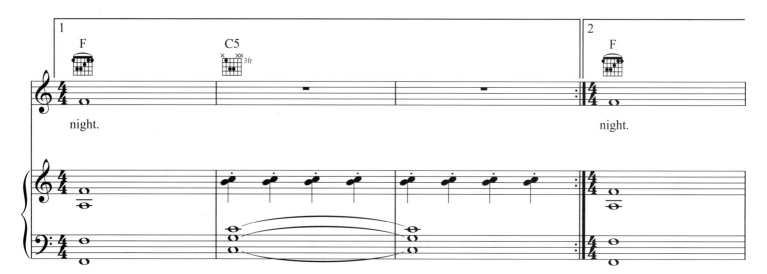

1   F   C5   2   F

night.   night.

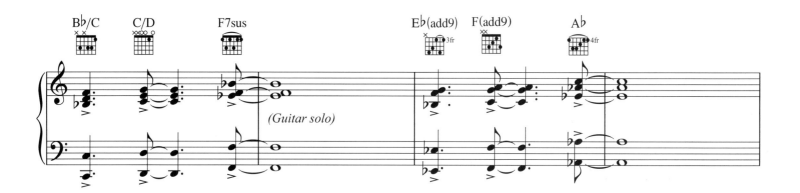

B♭/C   C/D   F7sus   E♭(add9)   F(add9)   A♭

(Guitar solo)

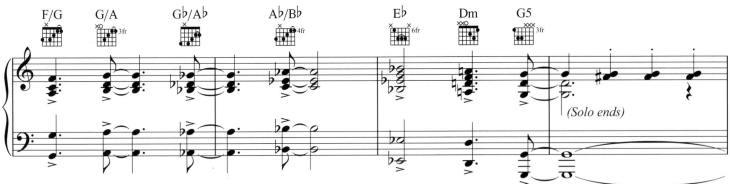

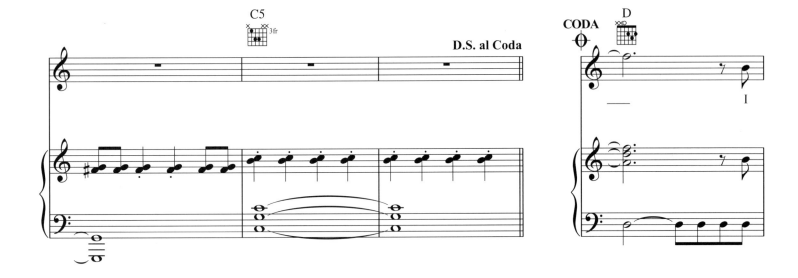

need your in - spi - ra - tion to-night. _ Blonde o - ver blue, _

_ your hands are cold, _ your eyes are fire. _ Blonde o - ver blue, _

they ____ shine as though you're burn-ing in - side. ____

One word from you ____ is all I need ____ to be in - spired. ____

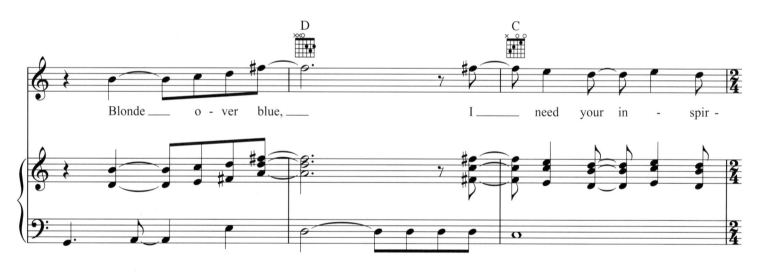

Blonde ____ o - ver blue, ____ I ____ need your in - spir -

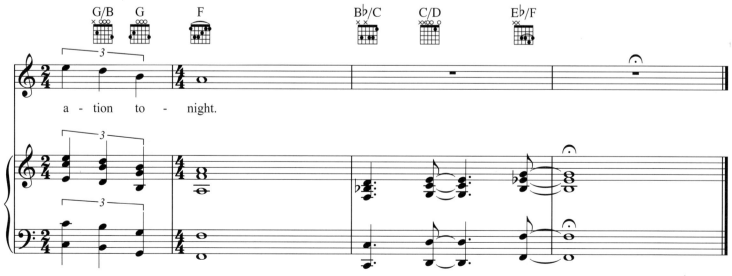

a - tion to - night.

A MINOR VARIATION

Words and Music by
BILLY JOEL

Moderately, smoothly

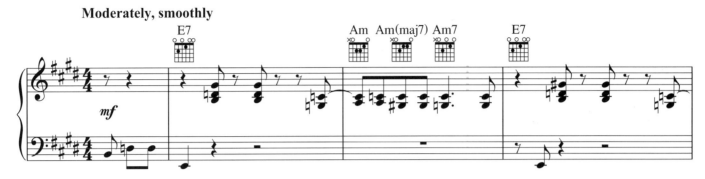

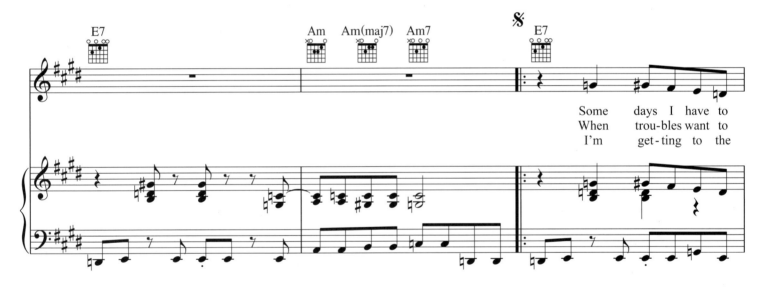

Some days I have to
When trou-bles want to
I'm get-ting to the

give right in to the blues.
find me, I ain't hard to find.
point where I don't feel the pain,

Des-pite how I try
They know where I am
and I've had e-nough.

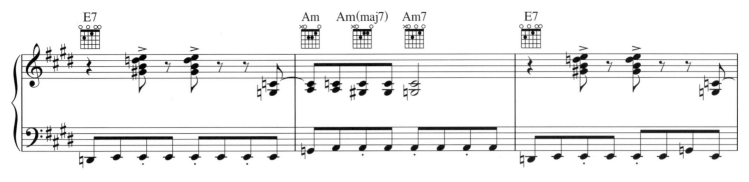

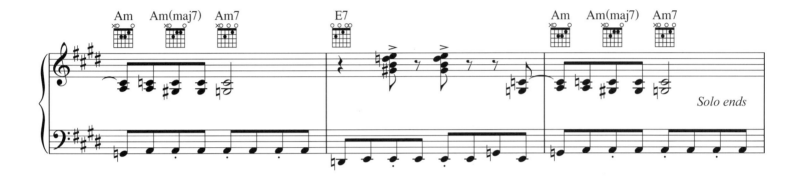

Solo ends

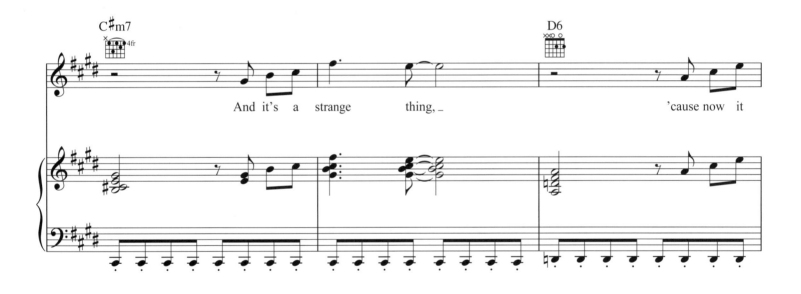

And it's a strange thing, ___ 'cause now it

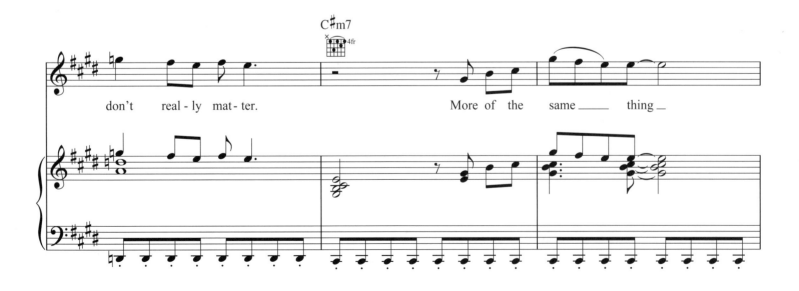

don't real-ly mat-ter. More of the same ___ thing ___

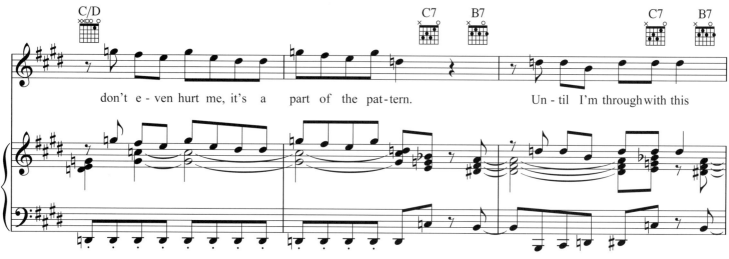

don't e - ven hurt me, it's a part of the pat-tern. Un - til I'm through with this

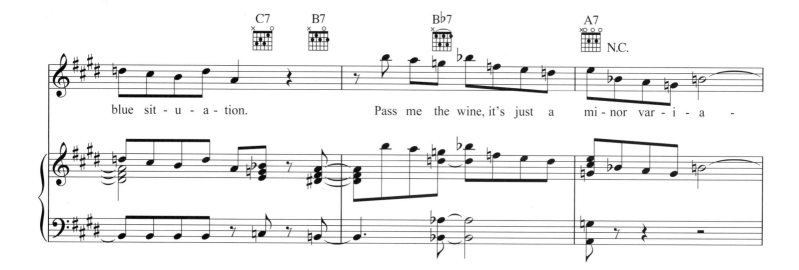

blue sit - u - a - tion. Pass me the wine, it's just a mi - nor var - i - a -

- tion. _____ Mi - nor var - i - a - tion. _

Repeat with ad libs and Fade

SHADES OF GREY

Words and Music by
BILLY JOEL

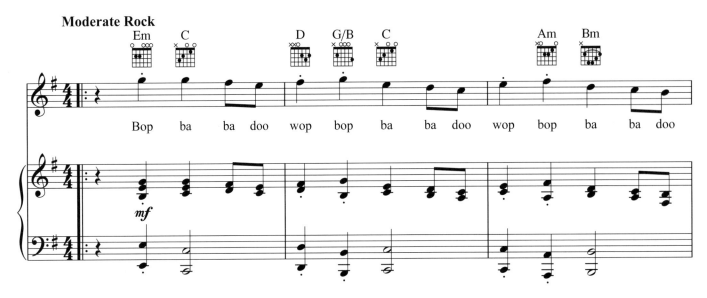

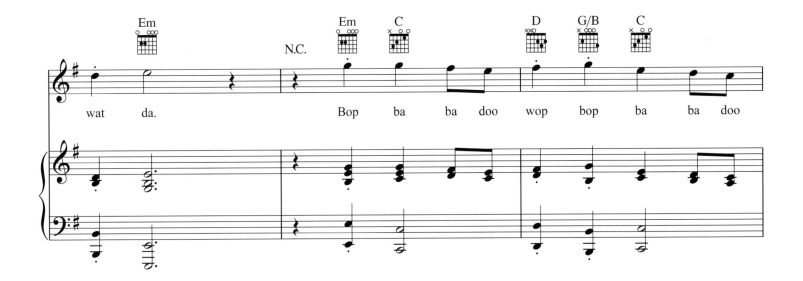

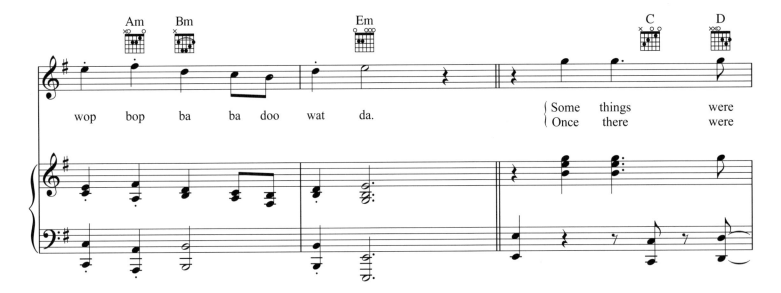

These alternate chords are played 2nd time.

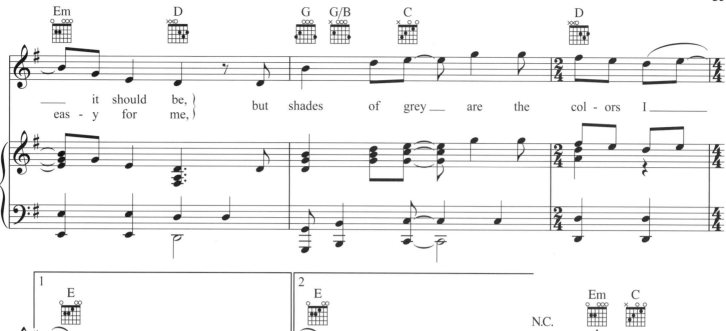

_____ it should be, }
eas - y for me, } but shades of grey ___ are the col - ors I _____

1
___ see.

2
___ see.

N.C.
Bop ba ba doo

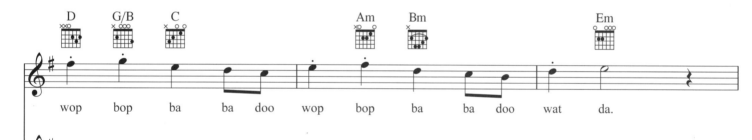

wop bop ba ba doo wop bop ba ba doo wat da.

N.C.
Bop ba ba doo wop bop ba ba doo wop bop ba ba doo

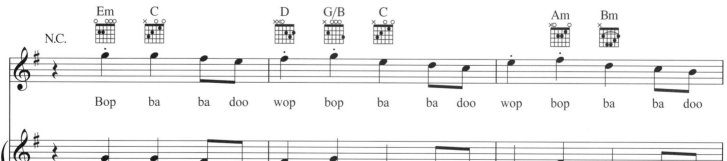

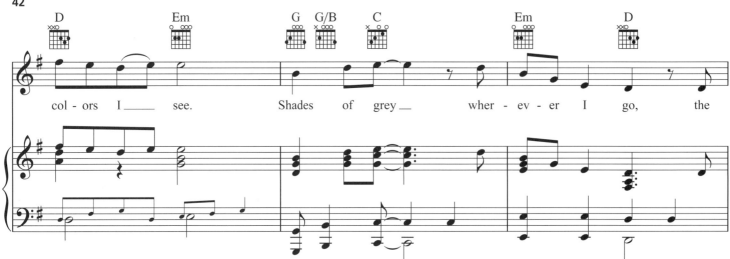

col - ors I ___ see. Shades of grey __ wher - ev - er I go, the

more I find __ out, the less that I __ know. There ain't no rain - bows shin -

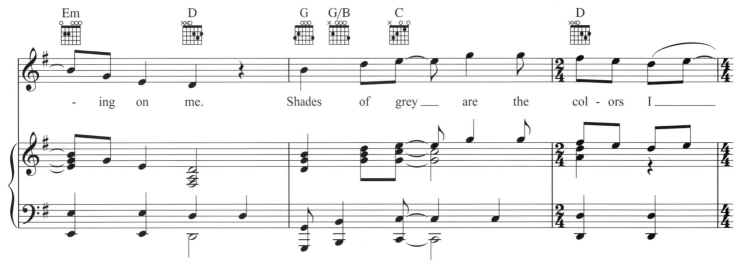

- ing on me. Shades of grey __ are the col - ors I _____

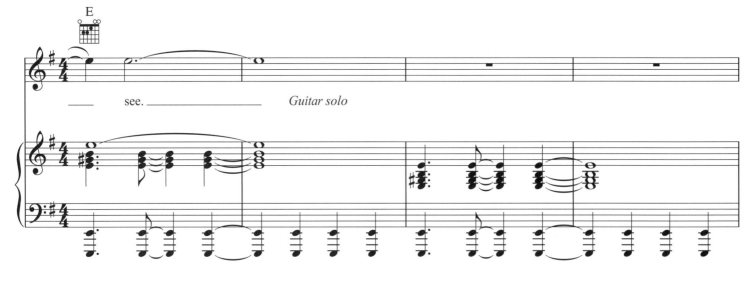

__ see. _____ *Guitar solo*

Solo ends

ALL ABOUT SOUL

Words and Music by
BILLY JOEL

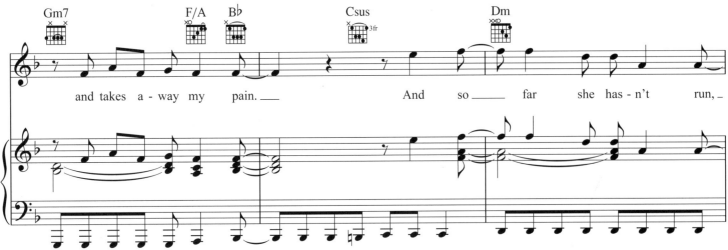

and takes a-way my pain. ___ And so ___ far she has-n't run, ___

___ though I swear she's ___ had ___ her mo-ments she

still be-lieves ___ in mir - a - cles while oth-ers cry in vain. ___

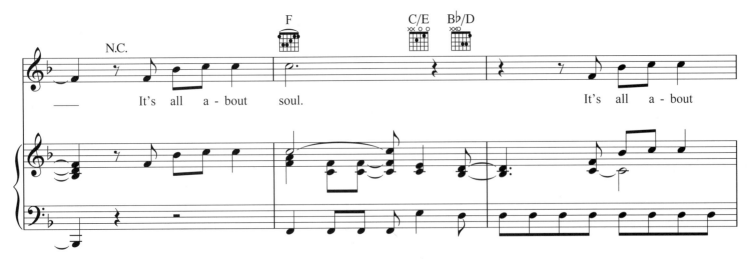

___ It's all a-bout soul. It's all a-bout

faith and a deep-er de-vo-tion. It's all a-bout soul. _____

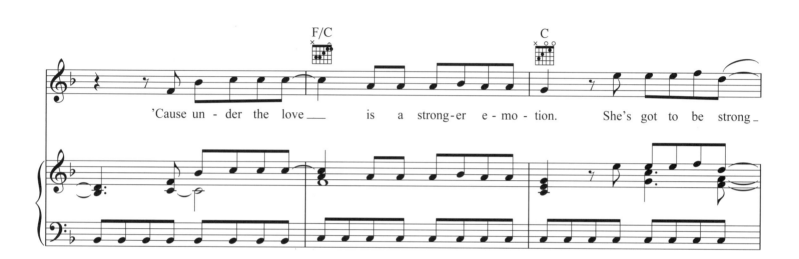

'Cause un-der the love ___ is a strong-er e-mo-tion. She's got to be strong _

_____ 'cause so man-y things ___ get-ting out of con-trol _

_____ should drive her a-way. Why does she stay? It's all a-bout

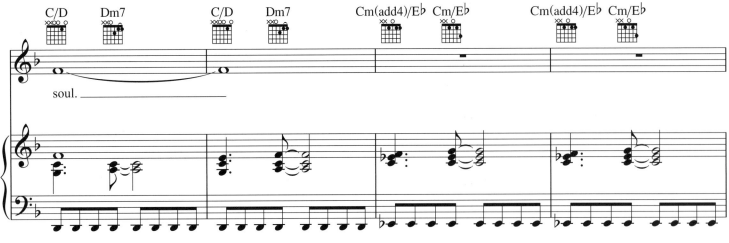

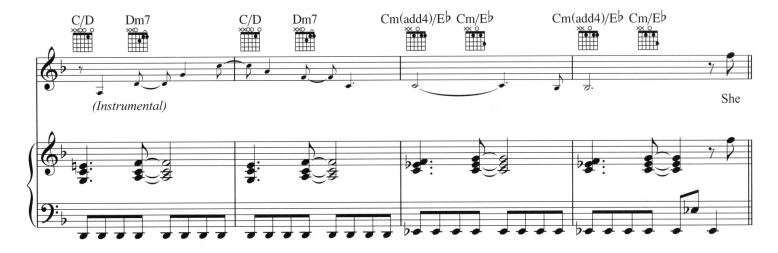

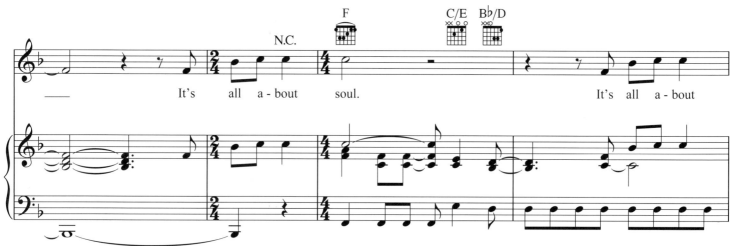

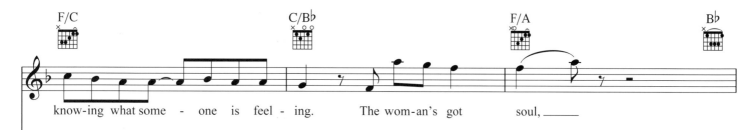

fair. _____ It's gon-na get dark, _____ it's gon-na get cold. _____

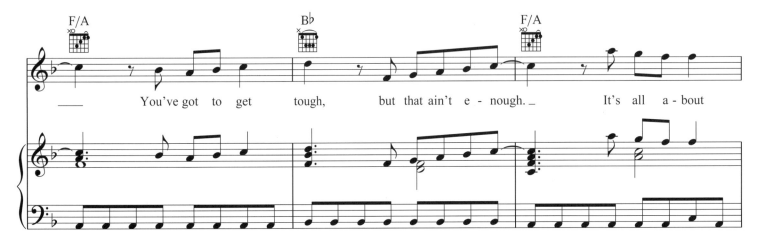

_____ You've got to get tough, but that ain't e-nough. _____ It's all a-bout

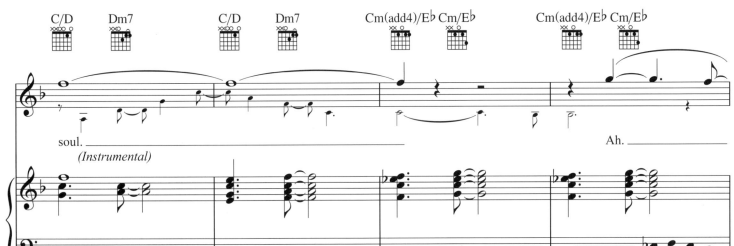

soul. _____ (Instrumental) Ah. _____

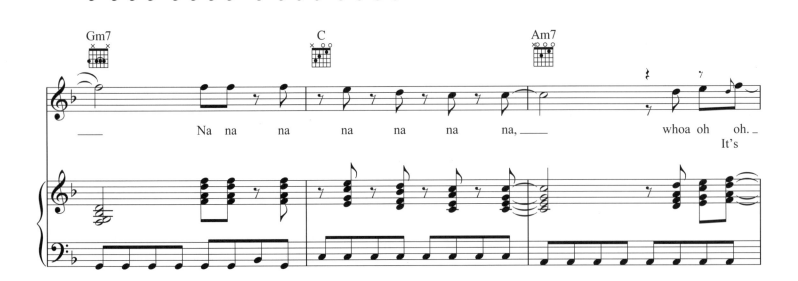

_____ Na na na na na na na, _____ whoa oh oh. _____ It's

all a-bout soul, _____ Na na na na na na na. _____ yes it is. _

_ Na na na na na na na, _____ whoa oh oh. _ It's

all a-bout soul _____ Na na na na na na na. _____

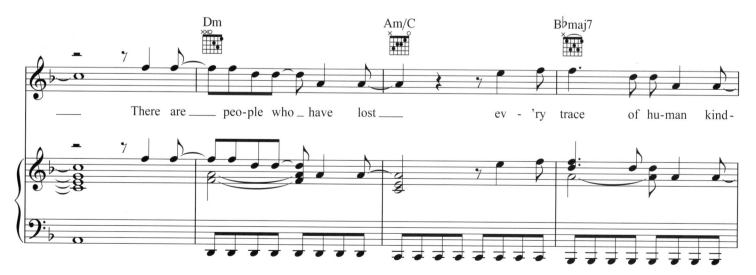

_ There are __ peo-ple who _ have lost __ ev-'ry trace of hu-man kind-

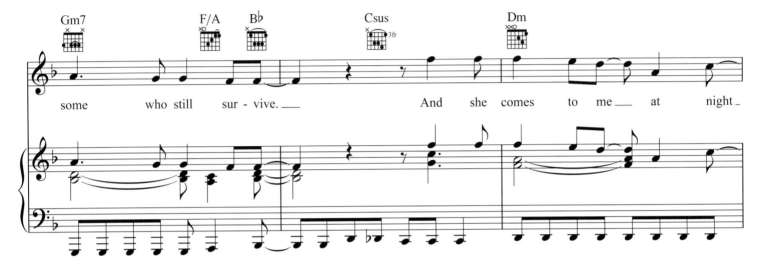

soul. It's all a-bout joy that comes_ out of sor-

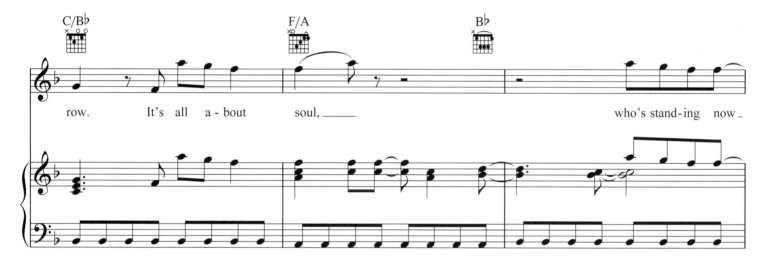

row. It's all a-bout soul,_____ who's stand-ing now_

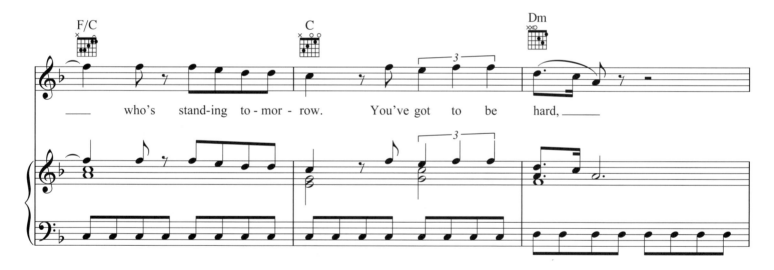

___ who's stand-ing to-mor-row. You've got to be hard,_____

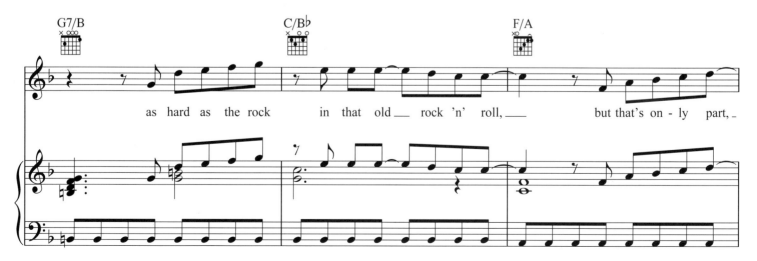

as hard as the rock in that old_ rock 'n' roll, ___ but that's on-ly part, _

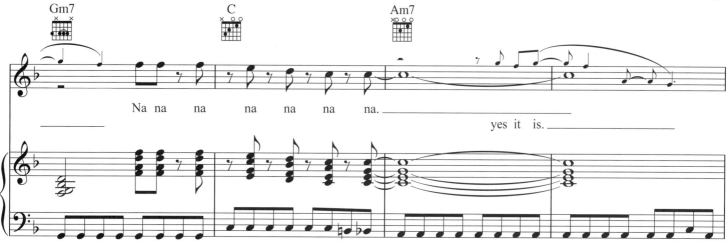

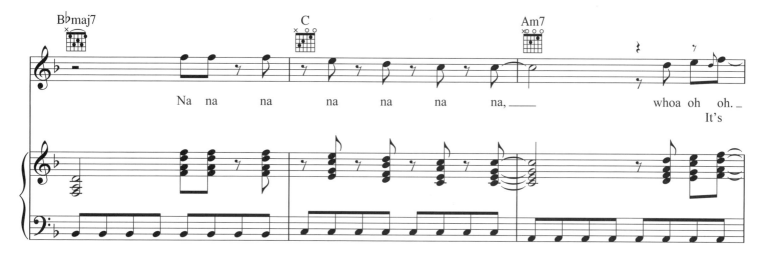

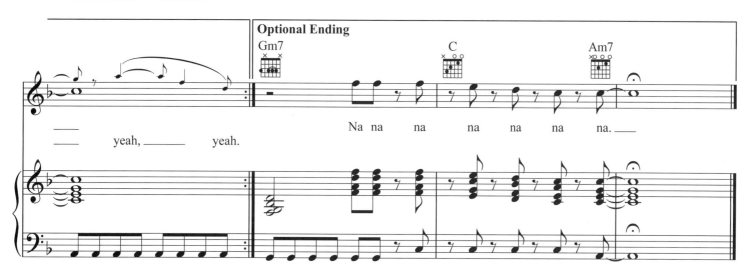

LULLABYE
(Goodnight, My Angel)

Words and Music by
BILLY JOEL

Rubato, gently

Good-night, my an - gel, time to close ___ your eyes and save these ques - tions for an- oth - er ___ day. I think I know what you've ___ been ask - ing me. I think you know ___ what I've ___ been trying to say. I prom-ised I ____ would nev - er

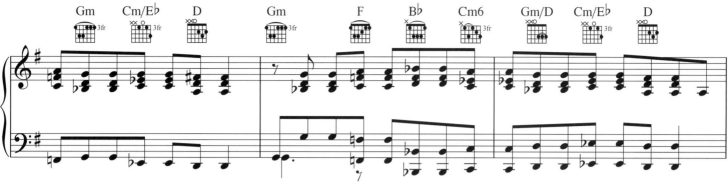

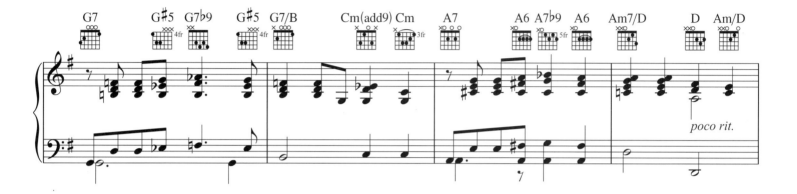

Good-night, my an - gel, now it's time to dream, and dream how won - der - ful __ your

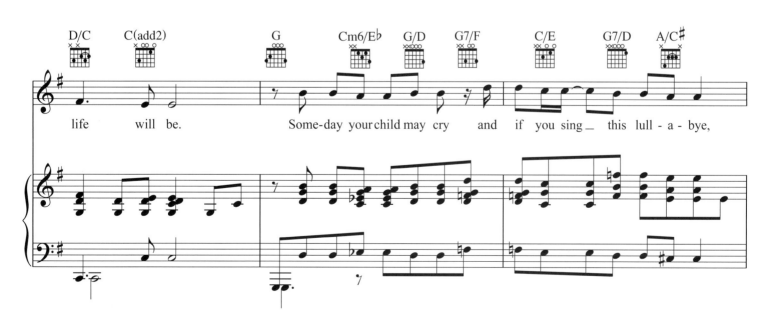

life will be. Some-day your child may cry and if you sing __ this lull - a - bye,

then in your heart there will al - ways be a part of me.

Some - day we'll all ___ be gone ___ but

lull - a - byes ___ go on ___ and on. They nev - er die, that's how you and ___ I will

be. ___

THE RIVER OF DREAMS

Words and Music by
BILLY JOEL

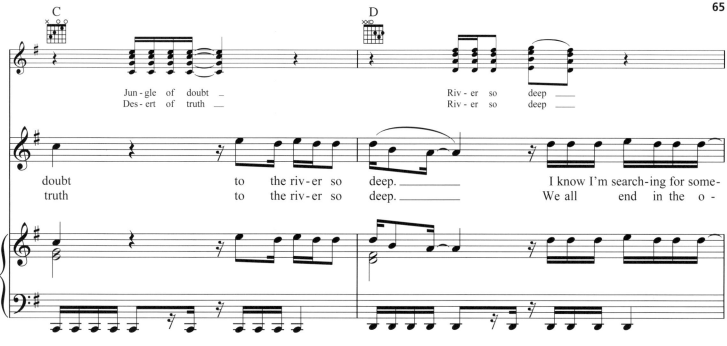

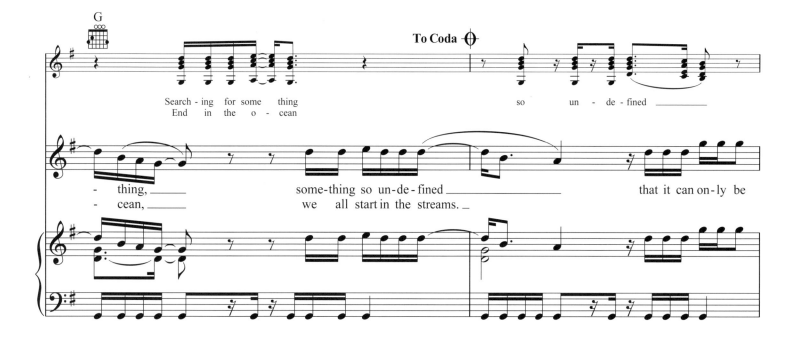

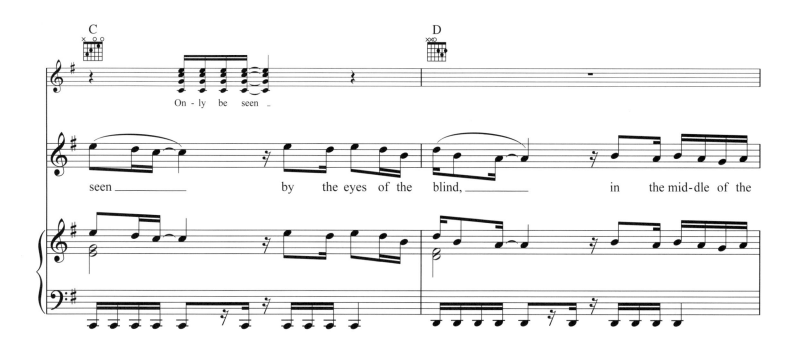

I go walk-ing in the in the mid-dle of a I go walk-ing in the in the mid-dle of a

night. ___
(Piano solo)

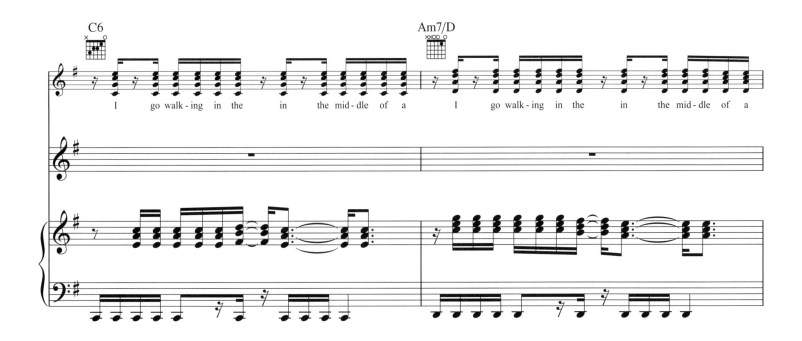

I go walk-ing in the in the mid-dle of a I go walk-ing in the in the mid-dle of a

I go walk-ing in the in the mid-dle of a I go walk-ing in the in the mid-dle of a

I go walk-ing in the in the mid-dle of a I go walk-ing in the in the mid-dle of a

(Solo ends)

I'm not sure a-bout a life af - ter this, God knows I've nev-er been a spir - i-tual man.

Bap - tized by the fire, I wade in-to the riv-er that is run-nin' to the prom-ised land.

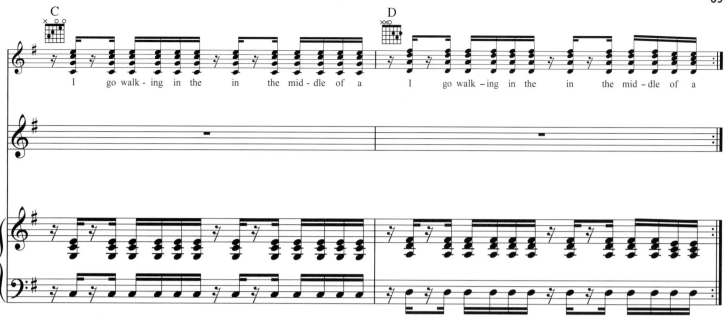

I go walk-ing in the in the mid-dle of a I go walk-ing in the in the mid-dle of a

I go walk-ing in the in the mid-dle of a I go walk-ing in the in the mid-dle of a

Lead vocal ad lib.

Repeat and Fade

I go walk-ing in the in the mid-dle of a I go walk-ing in the in the mid-dle of a

TWO THOUSAND YEARS

Words and Music by
BILLY JOEL

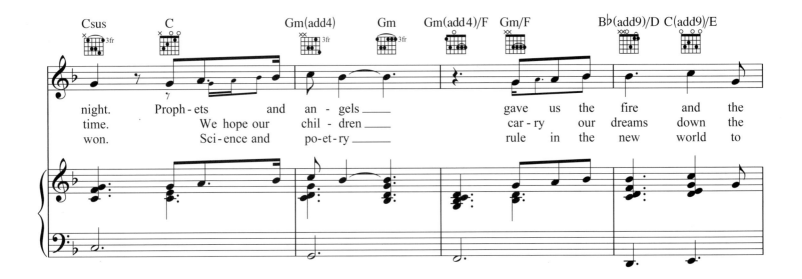

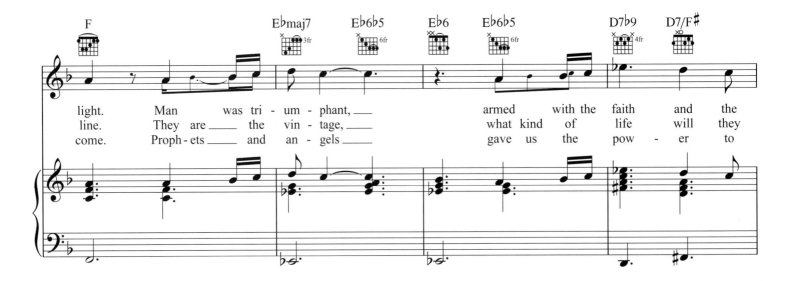

To Coda ⊕

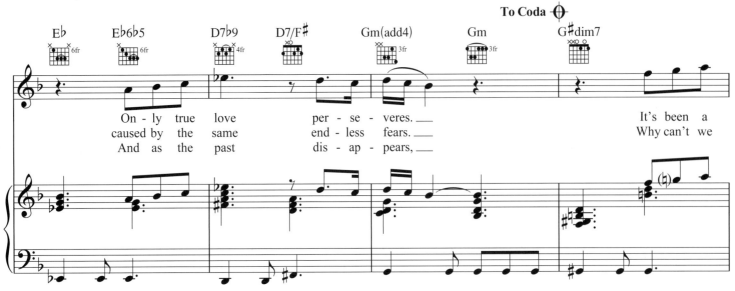

On - ly true love per - se - veres. ___ It's been a
caused by the same end - less fears. ___ Why can't we
And as the past dis - ap - pears, ___

long time and now, I'm ___ with you, af - ter two thou - sand
learn from all we've ___ been through, af - ter two thou - sand

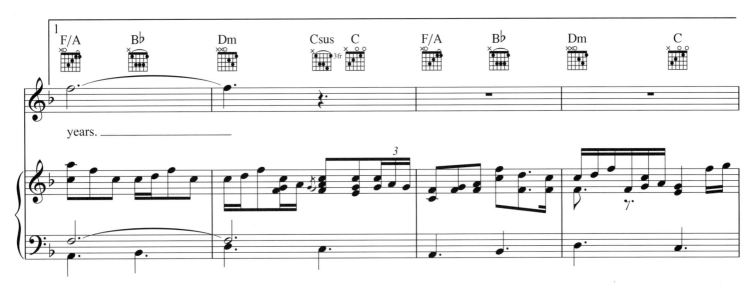

years. ___

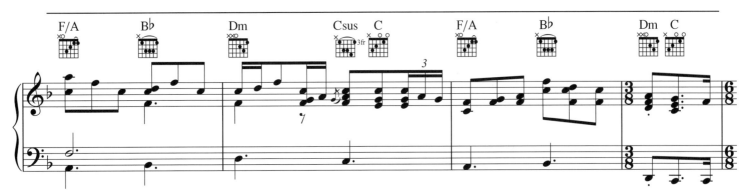

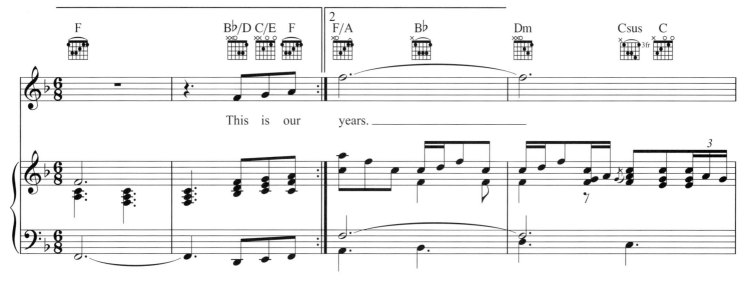

This is our years.

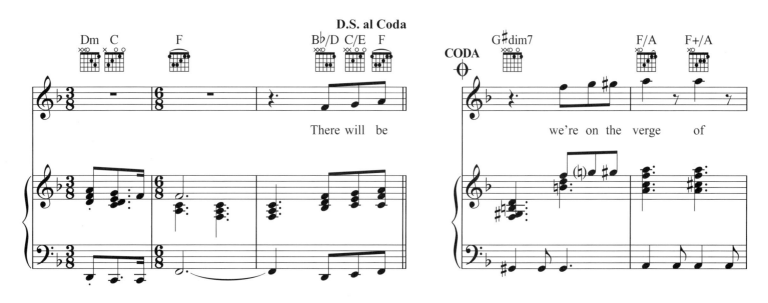

D.S. al Coda

There will be

CODA

we're on the verge of

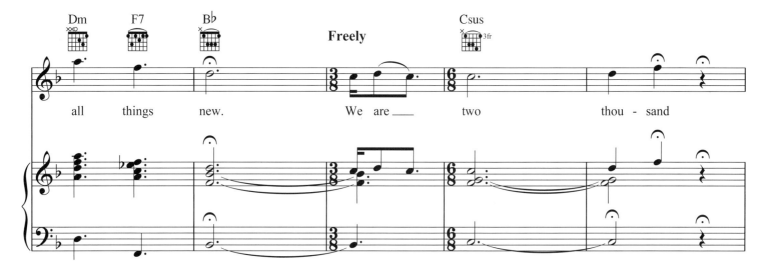

all things new. We are ___ two thou - sand

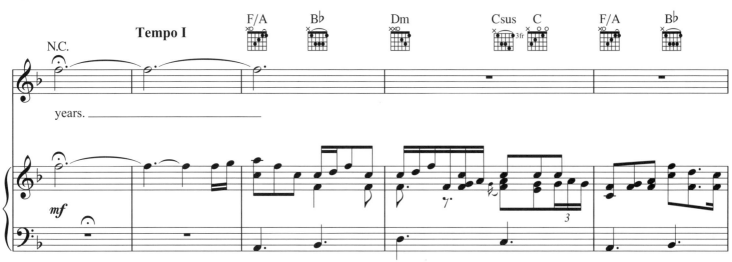

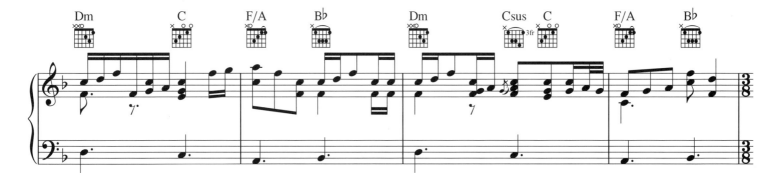

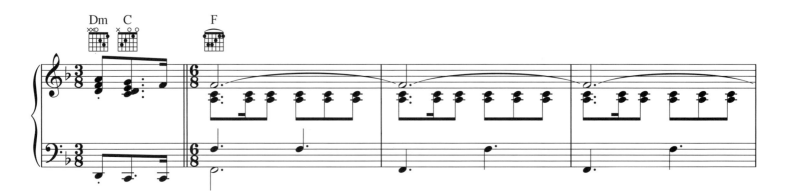

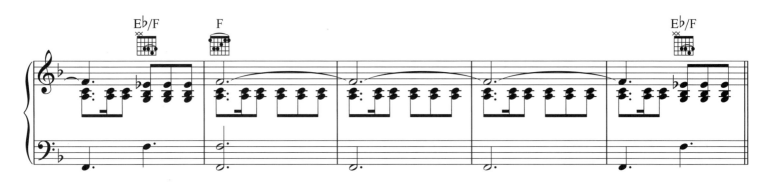

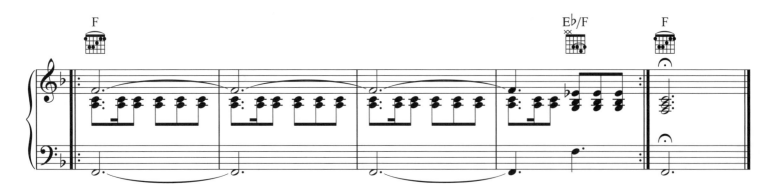

FAMOUS LAST WORDS

Words and Music by
BILLY JOEL

Moderate Rock

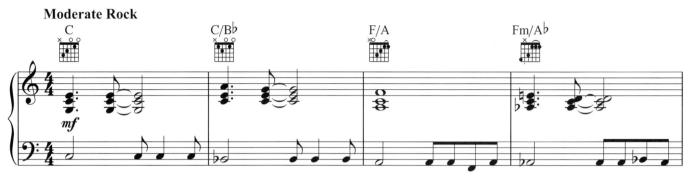

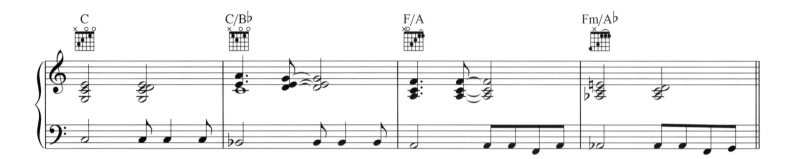

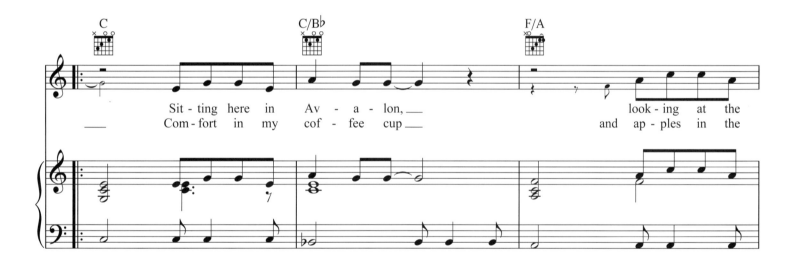

Sit - ting here in Av - a - lon, _____ look - ing at the
Com - fort in my cof - fee cup _____ and ap - ples in the

pour - ing rain. _____ Sum - mer - time has come and gone _____
ear - ly fall. _____ they're pull - ing all the moor - ings up _____

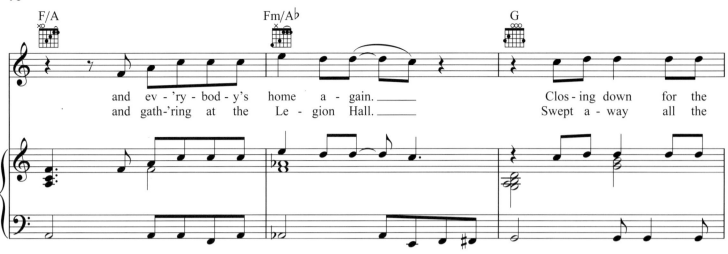

and ev-'ry-bod-y's home a - gain. _____ Clos-ing down for the
and gath-'ring at the Le - gion Hall. _____ Swept a - way all the

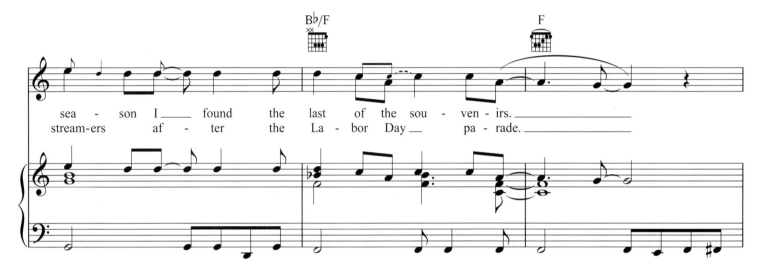

sea - son I _____ found the last of the sou - ven-irs. _____
stream-ers af - ter the La - bor Day _____ pa - rade. _____

I can still taste the wed-ding cake and it's sweet af - ter all these
There's noth-ing left for a dream - er now, on - ly one fi - nal ser - e -

years. _____ These are the last words _ I
nade. _____ And these are the last words _ I

have to say, _____ that's why it took_
have to say _____ be - fore an - oth -

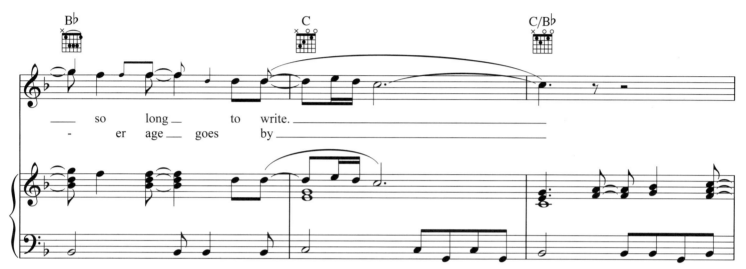

___ so long___ to write. _____
- er age___ goes by _____

There will be oth - er words ___ some oth - er ___ day, _____
with all those oth - er songs ___ I have to play, _____

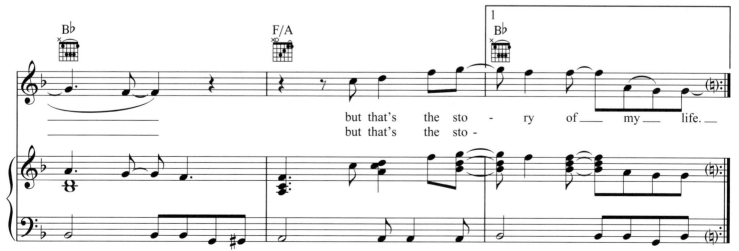

_____
but that's the sto - ry of ___ my ___ life. __
but that's the sto -

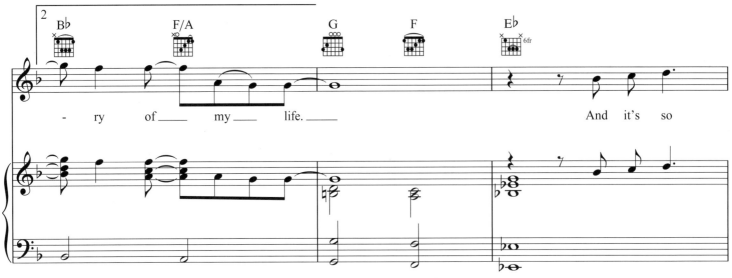

-ry of ___ my ___ life. ___ And it's so

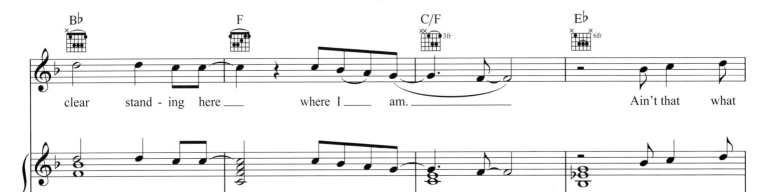

clear stand - ing here ___ where I ___ am. _____ Ain't that what

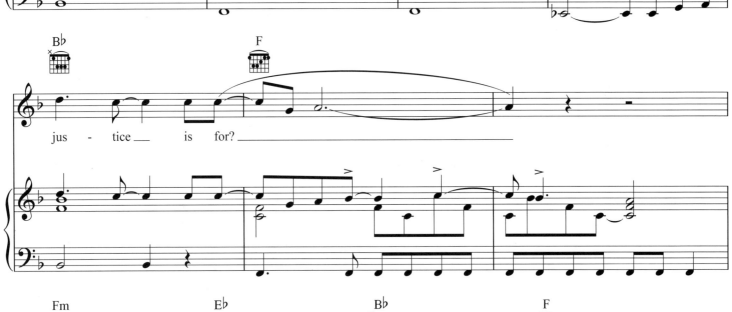

jus - tice ___ is for? _____

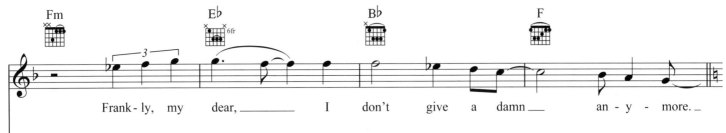

Frank - ly, my dear, ___ I don't give a damn ___ an - y - more. __

(Piano solo)

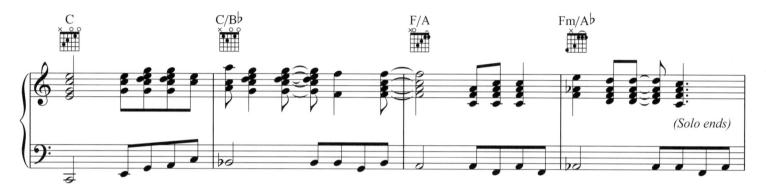

(Solo ends)

Stack the chairs on the ta - ble tops, __ hang the sheets on the chan - de - liers. __

It slows down, but it nev - er stops. __ Ain't it

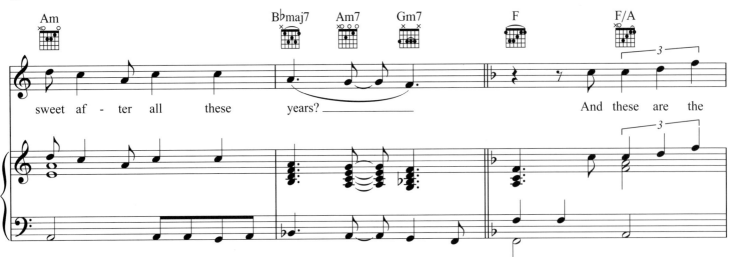

sweet af - ter all these years? _____ And these are the

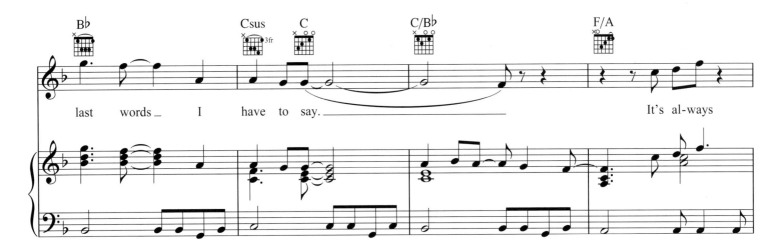

last words __ I have to say. _____ It's al-ways

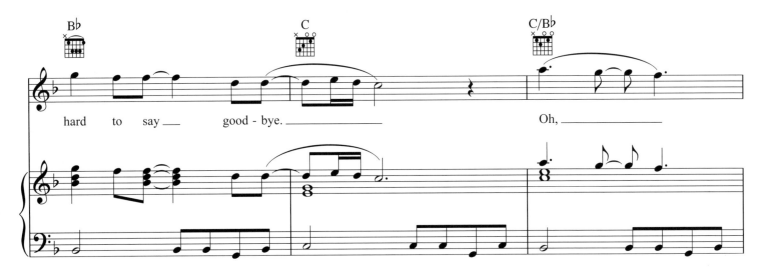

hard to say __ good - bye. _____ Oh, _____

but now it's time __ to put __ this book a - way. _____

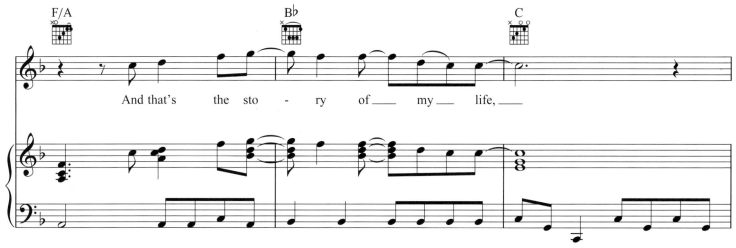

And that's the sto - ry of __ my __ life, __

oh. _____ These are the last words __ I have to say, _____

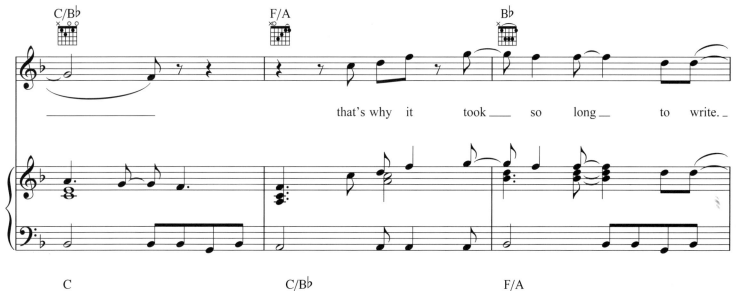

_____ that's why it took __ so long __ to write. _

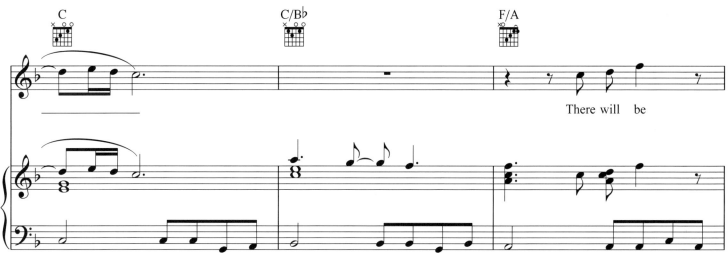

There will be

oth - er words _ some oth - er _ day, _____

ain't that the sto - ry of _ my _ life, _ oh. _____

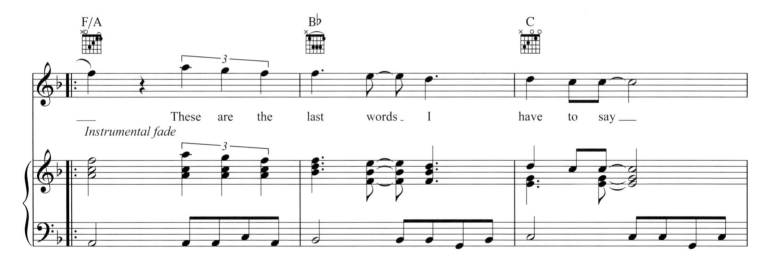

Instrumental fade

These are the last words _ I have to say _

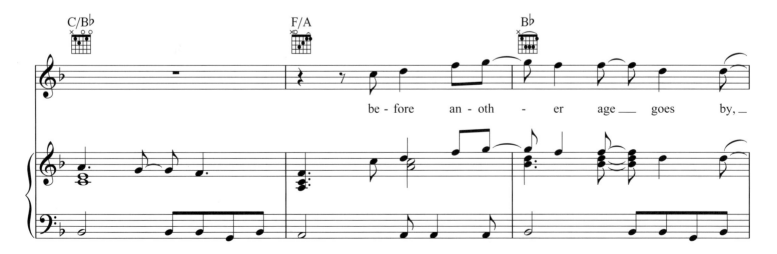

be - fore an - oth - er age _ goes by, _

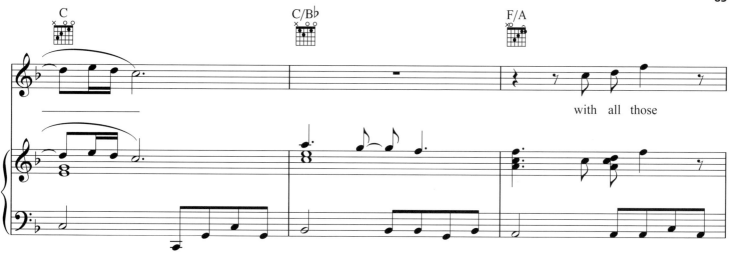

with all those

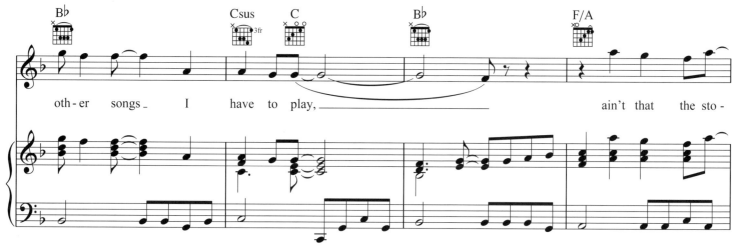

oth-er songs _ I have to play, _____ ain't that the sto-

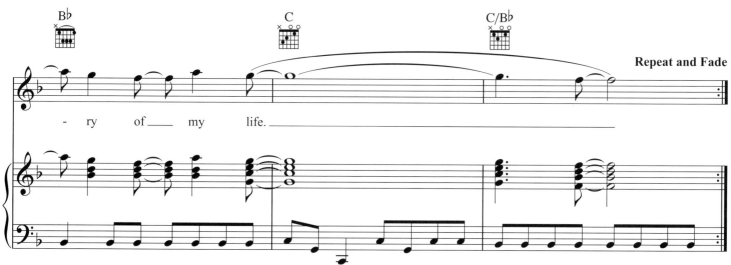

Repeat and Fade

-ry of ___ my life. _____

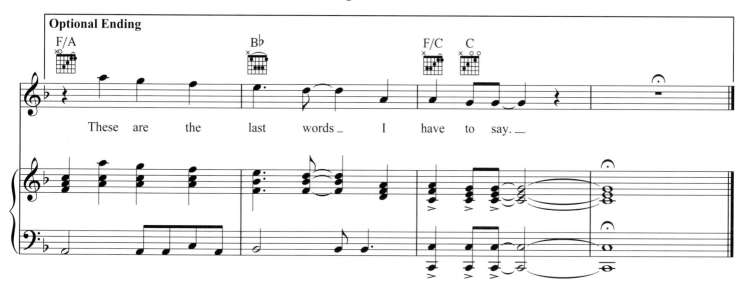

Optional Ending

These are the last words _ I have to say. _